Loon Laughter

Ecological Fables and Nature Tales

PAUL LEET AIRD

DRAWINGS BY THOREAU MacDONALD

EDITED BY CELINA OWEN

Copyright © 1997 by Paul Leet Aird and Carleton University Press.

Permission to use Thoreau MacDonald's drawings granted by the executrix of his estate.

Published by Carleton University Press with financial assistance from the Canada Council for the Arts, the Ontario Arts Council, and by the Government of Canada through the Department of Canadian Heritage and the Government of Ontario through the Ministry of Culture, Tourism and Recreation.

Printed and bound in Canada by Coach House Printing on Canadian acid-free and permanent paper, Rolland Opaque, Natural, Vellum Finish, 70 lb. with 20 per cent post-consumer fibre. The text font is Stempel Garamond.

The cover drawing by Thoreau MacDonald is from the cover of *The Literary Press Group Catalogue* Spring 1978, Toronto. The drawing on page vii was published by Thoreau MacDonald in *Woods and Fields*. Toronto: Ryerson Press, 1951. The drawing on page xiv was privately published by Thoreau MacDonald in *Birds & Animals*. Thornhill, Ontario: 1968.

CANADIAN CATALOGUING IN PUBLICATION DATA

Aird, Paul L.
    Loon laughter : ecological fables and nature tales

ISBN 088629-334-0

    1. Fables, Canadian (English) 2. Animals—Folklore. 3. Plants—Folklore. I. MacDonald, Thoreau, 1901- II. Owen, Celina III. Title.

PS8551.I75L66 1997   C813'.54   C97-901237-6
PR9199.3.A348L66 1997

DEDICATION

*for the wild animals, plants
and microorganisms I have known
for tramping and camping companions
for past, present and future generations*

ACKNOWLEDGEMENTS

My heartfelt thanks to family and friends for their help, encouragement and editorial advice – Margaret Aird, Diana Aird, Lyn Aird Barsevskis, Paul, Mark and Peter Barsevskis, Joan Aird Jacobsen, Deane Nesbitt, Jr., Linda Rean Pim, Don Pope, Janette Baker, Susan Greenwood, Fred Keenan, Hope Coxon, Beverley Cram, Forrest Buckingham, Julia Lee, Mark Stabb, Mercedes Ballem, Erin Nixon, Wendy Ripmeester, Leanne Leith, Kate Frego, Peter Timmerman, Arch and Helen Jones, Celina and Kalifa Owen, Anne Hansen, Henry Kock, Virgil Duff, Don Lake, the executrix of Thoreau MacDonald's estate, and many helpful reference librarians and art curators. I also acknowledge the help and encouragement of John Flood, Director of Carleton University Press, who shares with me a long-standing interest in the life and art of Thoreau MacDonald.

Published Fables:
  "The Acorn and the Oak Tree" *Policy Options* 9(6):47, 1988. *Forestry Chronicle* 64(5): 398, 1988. "The Lifeline" *The Globe and Mail*, Toronto, p.A7, October 3, 1989. CBC-TV Toronto, October 4, 1989. CBC-Radio, Thunder Bay, October 5, 1989. CBC-Radio, Toronto, October 8, 1989. *The Enterprise-Bulletin*, Collingwood, p.5A, January 27, 1990.

Two forces shape the world – nature and human nature.

CONTENTS

Preface x

A Letter to Thoreau MacDonald xiv

The Frog and the Fly 1
The Bison Jump 3
Last Prize 5
The Salmon Smolt 7
Scarecrow Jig 9
The King and the Royal Trees 11
The Farmer and the Bobolinks 13
Boulder Creek 15
Wolf Island 17
The Smart Ones 21
Cheer Up, Cheer Up 23
The Taste Test 27
The Acorn and the Oak Tree 29
Hawk Haven 33
V-Formation 35
Concrete Thinking 37
Mountain King 41
The Lifeline 43
Wilderness 45
Two Habitats 47
The Hawk and the Chickadee 49

The Hybrids 51
The Ploughers 53
The Winterberry Shrub 55
The Wolf Hunt 57
Polar Bear Reflections 59
Loon Laughter 61
Salmon Park 63
Survival 65
The Snake and the Cyclist 67
The Trilliums and the Bear 69
Caribou Crossing 71
Taddle Pond 73

Loon Laughter Activities, Celina Owen 77

Biography of Paul Leet Aird 83
Biography of Thoreau MacDonald (1901-1989) 84
Biography of Celina Owen 86

Emblems Drawn and Printed by Thoreau MacDonald 87

PREFACE

Loon Laughter is a book of fables and tales written about Canada's wild plants and animals, from an ecological perspective. It presents a suite of images of people and nature interacting in the Canadian landscape.

The traditional fable is a short fictitious story, written in prose or verse. It leads to a single and obvious conclusion that is designed to teach a moral or practical lesson in a creative or amusing way. It consists of two connected parts – the story and the moral – which may be likened to the wolf and its howl. In some fables, the moral is intertwined through the story. In others, the moral is prominently expressed as a proverb at the end or the beginning of the text.

Fables have a long oral and written tradition. Æsop's fables were created by a Greek slave about 600 B.C.; the Indian Jataka tales were first collected and recorded in 500 B.C. In the first century A.D., the Roman Phaedrus wrote fables in Latin verse. The Indian Panchatantra tales were recorded about the 3rd century A.D.

Later fabulists include Marie de France in the twelfth century (her gods were always female); the French fabulist Jean de La Fontaine in the seventeenth century; John Gay of England and Gotthold Lessing of Germany in the eighteenth century; Ivan Krylov of Russia and the Afro-American "Uncle Remus" fables in the ninteenth century; and the humorous fables by American writers Mark Twain in the ninteenth century and James Thurber and E.B. White in this century.

Their fables are often misclassified as "children's literature." In fact, most of these fables were written for adults as social and political statements or satires appropriate to their times. The French fabulist Jean de La Fontaine wrote to His Royal Highness the Dauphin that Æsop's fables were "simplicities cloaking what in truth is profound."

Fables thrive on brevity and simplicity. Gotthold Lessing's *Essay on Fable* (1759) emphasizes that "brevity is the soul of fable and that its greatest ornament is to have none at all." The great fabulists avoid description or compassionate narrative that might obscure the perception of moral truth. Simplicity was paramount.

Though many fabulists have written about humans, the preferred characters are animals, plants, the sun, moon, stars, mythical gods or natural forces such as the wind and fire. The heroes and villains of fables are many: wolf, lamb, fox, crow, lion, mouse, sun, moon, oak, fir, frog, crab, hare, tortoise, ant, grasshopper, wasp ... the list goes on.

These non-human characters help to maintain the simplicity of the fable. In a fable, a wolf is always a wolf and a fox is always a fox. We do not need a description of size, colour, age or temperament to distinguish between them. Instead, we know or learn that the wolf always has long fangs, and the fox is always clever (sometimes too clever), that the owl is always wise, and the tortoise always slow and steady.

In the traditional fable, however, animals represented humans. In *Loon Laughter*, the animals represent themselves. These fables attempt to build on Canada's literary tradition of depicting wild animals from the animals' perspective. While early British writers of animal stories concentrated on animal fantasies, and American writers on animal conquests, the early Canadian writers published realistic animal stories based on personal observations of wildlife behaviour.

The stories in *Loon Laughter* combine the realistic animal story with the fable form. They are ecological stories, based on personal observation, study and research of wild animals and plants.

In these ecological stories, animals and plants are depicted in a variety of natural or unnatural environments and are able to demonstrate and explain their own points of view. They act as themselves and not as people, or superior beings because they can speak. They often interact with humans, for humans both cause and solve the environmental problems faced by plants and animals.

We know that plants and animals can communicate with one another. Perhaps Canada's spectacular heritage of wild plants and animals can communicate with people too, through the medium of these words and Thoreau MacDonald's exquisite line drawings.

Paul Aird, November 1997
Inglewood, Ontario

LINE DRAWING[1]

Line drawing has one advantage over other means of graphic expression. It's cheaper to print. But it's limited, troublesome to execute, and to most people has little interest compared to halftone or color. It's possible by very fine lines and other forms of minute penwork to almost equal a halftone or photo. But this is more or less a degradation of true line drawing, which should be marked by the apparent simplicity and decision of a well handled ax or scythe.

A line drawing is something like a blueprint or like shorthand; it has its symbols and conventions and these should be accepted to get its meaning. The draftsman tries, with these few marks and lines, to indicate all the forms and colours of land, water and sky, humans and animals, buildings, rocks, trees and snow, the variations in spruce and cedar, granite and limestone, elm and maple. He may use black areas, outline, parallel lines, cross-hatching and white paper; but with these elements he tries to represent the visible world.

The present drawings are shown only as a few chips left after thirty years of hacking away at the problems of line drawing. They are feeble reminders of reality, the farms and woods, swamps and brush of the author's native country.

Thoreau MacDonald, January 1952
Thornhill, Ontario

[1] Preface written for an exhibition of two hundred of Thoreau MacDonald's drawings at the London Public Library and Art Museum, London, Ontario, 1952. Preface held in file "Shelf 038 Thoreau MacDonald unmatted," Agnes Etherington Art Centre, Queen's University, Kingston, Ontario.

A LETTER TO THOREAU MacDONALD

"These drawings are a kind of record of meetings with animals. They are not the work of a naturalist nor an artist just a fond observer." T.M. Thornhill, 1968

Dear Thoreau,

    Over the years I have collected some of your books of drawings and writings, other books illustrated by you, and a few of your original drawings. I have become a Thoreau MacDonald fan.

    In my judgement, you are an exceptional Canadian artist, designer, illustrator and writer. Your black-and-white drawings of "birds and animals" in their natural habitats are truly thrilling to see.

    The Thomas Fisher Rare Book Library at the University of Toronto maintains a fine collection of your sketches, drawings, paintings and other works. Many of the species you have drawn are the prime actors in my fables, and some of your drawings have stimulated new stories.

    As I wrote these fables for *Loon Laughter*, I hoped that someone of your calibre would illustrate them. Later, I had a revelation: Perhaps I could obtain permission to use your illustrations to complement my fables. I asked the adminstrator of your estate and the answer was "Yes."

    Your black-and-white drawings of plants and animals are among the best illustrations of the spirit of Canada's north of all artists I know. I am delighted that your exquisite drawings will grace *Loon Laughter*. They will help greatly to persuade our readers to pause and reflect on the "concepts of Nature expressed in the limitations of paintings" and words.

    Yours in nature,

    Paul

Black-and-white drawing
From *Canadian Bookman* (1939) and from
Birds and Animals (1971),
second series, Thoreau MacDonald, privately published

THE FROG AND THE FLY

A NORTHERN LEOPARD FROG sat on the bank of the pond. He was very hungry. Water and air pollution were killing many insects, which made it difficult for him to find enough food to eat.

A bright green fly landed on a rusty woodsia fern beside the frog.

"You are a handsome fly," the frog croaked. "What kind of fly are you?"

"I am a blowfly and I am quite clever," it buzzed. "I know all about water pollution. It hurts some living things but it does not hurt me, so it is not harmful. It is the same with air pollution. It hurts some things but it does not hurt me, so it is not harmful. I know all about frogs, too. Your tongue is not long enough to reach me, so you are not harmful."

The frog took a long jump, caught the fly with his tongue, and ate it.

Black-and-white drawing
From *Woods and Fields* (1951), Thoreau MacDonald,
Ryerson Press, Toronto

THE BISON JUMP

Thousands of bison moved across the prairie, earthy brown against a shimmering expanse of green and gold. Some of the bison chewed sedately on tall prairie grasses while flies buzzed lazily among them. Others dozed in the mid-day sun, their woolly coats soaking up the heat. A few calves gambolled close to their mothers, whose resonant lowing reminded them to stay near. Several bulls rested, watchful, on the herd's fringes.

A sudden bellow broke the peace. An old bull, insane from a festering battle wound, stamped around, tossing his head wildly. Then he began to run through the herd towards a nearby river, craving a drink of water.

Another huge bull bellowed at the stirring herd as he ran after the first. A third madly pursued the leaders. They trampled the swaying grasses as they ran on.

The rest of the bison were some distance back. As the massive herd picked up speed, the animals' hooves striking the thick prairie sod sounded like muffled thunder. The stampede shook the earth and reverberated across the land and down the steep-sided river valley.

In desperation to reach the river, the lead bison ran toward a cliff that dropped straight to the valley below. Suddenly, he jumped off the cliff and fell to his death. Ignorant of the danger ahead, and following too closely to escape the same fate, the second bison also hurtled off the cliff. The third followed the others to its death.

A female bison approached the cliff more slowly. She saw the edge in time to turn and, choosing instead a gently sloping path down into the valley, led the herd safely to the river to drink.

Black-and-white drawing
From *Woods and Fields* (1951), Thoreau MacDonald, Ryerson Press, Toronto

LAST PRIZE

The fairy slipper orchids were the most beautiful flowers growing in the spruce bog. They blossomed in springtime and early summer. Each orchid had richly coloured pinkish-purple sepals and petals that surrounded a lavender slipper marked with thin red lines.

One spring, someone discovered the beautiful orchids, picked a few and took them home to show friends. From then on, people often visited the bog to see and photograph the lovely flowers. Many people picked the flowers, until only one clump remained.

One day a photographer discovered the last clump of fairy slipper orchids. Attracted by their rare beauty, he set up a camera on a tripod and focussed on the wild flowers. "Nature photographers never disturb the natural habitat," he said to himself as he cut off an unsightly spruce branch that drooped low over the orchids. He looked through the lens again and then pulled out five of the older, faded orchids, even though they had been pollinated and were now setting seed that could become new plants next year.

Satisfied with the scene, the photographer snapped the shutter and exclaimed, "I have just taken the picture of a lifetime. It will be an award-winning nature photograph."

He leaned down to admire the flowers once more and then picked them so no one else could take such a beautiful picture. As he left the spruce bog, he searched for other clumps to photograph but could not find any. The beautiful fairy slipper orchids wilting in his hand were all that remained.

Black-and-white drawing
From *Mountain Cloud* (1944), Marius Barbeau,
Macmillan of Canada, Toronto

THE SALMON SMOLT

A SITKA SPRUCE TREE grew beside a river. Day after day, it watched the water flow toward the sea.

One day, the tree watched a young salmon swimming downstream and asked: "Where are you going?"

"I'm swimming down the river to the sea," said the salmon smolt. "I want to see the world and learn about everything around me."

"I can see the sea from here," the spruce tree replied proudly. "You don't need to swim any farther. I can answer all of your questions."

"What does it look like?" the salmon asked.

"The sea is just a strip of water beside some beautiful trees," said the spruce.

"How wide is the sea?" inquired the fish.

"I believe I can see across it on a clear day," the tree replied.

"Is the sea beautiful?" the young salmon asked eagerly.

"A sitka spruce tree growing beside the sea is prettier than the sea," the spruce replied truthfully.

A mountain goat overheard the discussion and said: "In the summertime, I climb up to the top of the mountain. I have seen the sea many times. The sea is just a strip of water beside a rocky cliff."

"How wide is the sea?" inquired the fish.

"I believe I can easily jump across it," the goat replied.

"Is the sea beautiful?" the young fish asked eagerly.

"A mountain goat leaping on the rocks beside the sea is prettier than the sea," the goat said truthfully.

A bald eagle joined the discussion: "Each day I soar high

above the mountain to feel the warmth of the sun. My eyes are keen. The sea is just a strip of water that meets the sky."

"How wide is the sea?" inquired the fish.

"I believe I can glide across the sea without flapping my wings," said the eagle.

"Is the sea beautiful?" the salmon smolt asked eagerly.

"An eagle soaring in the sky above the sea is prettier than the sea," the eagle said truthfully.

While the sitka spruce, the mountain goat and the bald eagle continued to observe the sea from afar, the smolt swam on to learn a salmon's truth about the sea.

Black-and-white drawing
From the cover of *Canadian Forum*, October 1930

SCARECROW JIG

A CROW LANDED ON A CORN STALK in front of a scarecrow. "Scarecrow," she cawed, "I remember last spring when you first appeared in this field. I was frightened by the way you waved your arms, and the way you twirled in the wind."

"Was I really that frightening?" asked the scarecrow, very pleased with itself.

"Yes, even your shadow frightened me," answered the crow. "At sunrise and at sunset, your shadow was very long, and the wind flowing through your hair whistled loudly. You frightened me so much I never landed in your field."

"I performed my job well!" exclaimed the scarecrow.

"Yes, but not now," laughed the crow. "I wonder why they call you a scarecrow. The corn plants are as tall as you are. You can no longer see me eating the corn."

"There is a time to scare and a time to share," said the scarecrow.

"What do you mean?" asked the crow.

"In the springime, when the corn seed was planted, I had to scare the birds away," said the scarecrow. "Otherwise, the birds would eat the seeds and there would not be a corn crop. Now the corn plants are tall and each corn cob is full. There is more than enough corn to feed you and your family, the farm family, and many more animals. I frighten you in the springtime and feed you in the fall."

The scarecrow was happy and began to dance a jig in the warm breeze. The crow flapped around the field while the scarecrow danced. When the jig ended, the crow flew down and perched on the scarecrow's shoulder.

"I love corn and I love scarecrows," cawed the crow.

Black-and-white drawing
From *West By East and Other Poems* (1933), J.E.H. MacDonald,
Ryerson Press, Toronto

THE KING AND THE ROYAL TREES

The king had a frightful dream. He dreamt that while riding his horse through the Royal Forest, the south wind called: "Beware of falling trees! Beware of falling trees!"

Though the trees were beautiful and waved gently in the wind, the King was frightened. He turned his horse and galloped out of the forest.

The next morning the King ordered his people to cut down all the trees in the kingdom. "We do not want the trees to fall down and hurt our children," he reasoned. "We will remove the forest and grow vegetables instead."

The people liked the King's idea, for now they had their pick of the finest wood in the forest to build houses and furniture, and the rest of the trees were sold at handsome prices to neighbouring kingdoms.

Once all of the trees were cut down, the King felt happy – and relieved. But the people were unhappy. They missed the trees, which had provided work for loggers and carpenters, and homes for birds. Although they sadly missed their work, they missed the birds most of all.

Soon after the trees were gone, a dry south wind began to blow. It blew day after day. The vegetable crops began to wither and die. People huddled helplessly in their houses watching the wind uproot their gardens and scatter the dead plants across the land.

The King was worried. He saddled his horse and rode through the fields to inspect the damage. There were no more trees to break the fury of the wind. As the wind blew faster, it swept withered plants and soil past the King, who watched silently as his kingdom blew northward.

Lost in clouds of dust and drifting sand, fatigue overcame the King. Nodding asleep in the saddle, he heard the south wind call: "Beware of falling trees! Beware of falling trees!"

Detail from the cover of *Canadian Forum,* May 1928

THE FARMER AND THE BOBOLINKS

A FARMER WAS CUTTING HAY to feed the animals on his farm. As he drove slowly through the field, a male bobolink began to fly round and round in front of the tractor.

The farmer knew why the bird was alarmed and slowed down. Suddenly a female bobolink flew up from her nest in the field. As quickly as possible, the farmer stopped the tractor.

He saw the female bobolink return swiftly to a patch of red clover where her nest was hidden. The agitated male still flew about.

The farmer did not get off his tractor to inspect the nest because that would disturb the young bobolinks. Instead, he pondered his dilemma. "If I cut around the nest, and leave some hay standing, people will call me a wasteful or messy farmer, but if I cut the field clean...." His thoughts trailed off and he shuddered.

With a slight smile, the farmer backed up his tractor. Very carefully, he drove around the bobolink nest, leaving lots of hay to keep the nest well hidden from predators.

Black-and-white drawing
From *Ontario's Future? Conservation or Else* (1952),
F.H. Kortright, Conservation Council of Ontario, Toronto

BOULDER CREEK

Clumps of moss grew on a boulder's weathered surface. Patches of lichen clung to its sides. Forest animals climbed on the boulder, slept beside it, hid behind it and dug beneath it. Surrounded by forest, the boulder had stood at the top of this slope for more than ten thousand years.

One day, an angler strode up to the boulder and pointed a fishing rod at it. "This one!" he called to the nearby tractor driver. As the angler moved away from the boulder, he said to himself, "This will definitely improve the fishing here."

The tractor pushed against the boulder until it began to roll down the slope. The stone smashed over small trees, tore bark off larger trees, destroyed a chipmunk hole and splashed into the stream. Then the tractor rolled more stones down the slope into the water. When he stopped, the driver looked uncertainly at the damage that had been done to the forest.

Noticing his concern, the angler assured the driver: "The trees and lichen will soon grow back. We need these stones to make new hiding and resting places for fish. Then we will put faster growing fish into the stream so it will be better for fishing than ever before."

The tractor moved to the top of the steep bank overhanging the stream. It began to push the soil into the water. This would make a smoother slope so it would be easier and safer for people to fish from the shore.

Suddenly, a kingfisher flew from the nest it had dug into the bank. It shrieked in alarm.

"Kingfishers are a real nuisance. They eat our fish," said the angler, with a wave of his arm. The tractor continued to scrape away the slope.

"We are wounding the forest," the tractor driver called above the noise of the engine.

"Nature heals its own wounds," the angler answered. "The seeds of different plants will blow in and germinate. Soon all will be green again."

"Nature might find a way to heal the wounds we are making to the stream, too," the driver warned.

"We are not wounding the stream. We are improving it," the angler insisted. "If nature changes what we have done, we will change it back. Anglers know what makes a good fishing spot."

A thunderstorm began to rumble in the west. Rain fell heavily. It continued for several days. As more and more water filled the stream, it flowed more and more quickly.

The boulders now in the stream restricted the flow of water and the stream overflowed its banks. The raging floodwaters filled in the old channel with sand and gravel, and carved a new channel for the stream on the other side of the valley.

Though the large boulder was almost buried, its top remained above the ground. The animals of the forest still climbed on the boulder, slept beside it, hid behind it and dug beneath it, as they had done before, and the kingfisher continued to nest close to the stream.

WOLF ISLAND

A LARGE ISLAND WAS HOME to many different species of animals. Each species had its own needs. The deer, rabbits, mice and chickadees fed on leaves, branches, buds and seeds. The wolves, snakes, hawks and owls fed on any animal they could catch.

The animals lived together in balance: when the number of rabbits increased, the number of wolves went up; when the number of rabbits decreased, the number of wolves went down.

In spite of this balanced relationship, the rabbits believed that their world would be more peaceful without the wolves. They always seemed to be hiding from wolves and watching out for wolves. They thought that if they could only scare the wolves off the island, life would be easier. But none of the rabbits was brave enough to try.

Then the rabbits developed a plan. They would ask the deer to help them chase the wolves off the island.

The next day, the deer and the rabbits lined up in a row and marched slowly across the island. The stags rattled their antlers together, which frightened the wolves. The rabbits ran in and out of the dense shrubs, to be certain that no wolves were hiding from the deer.

The deer chased the wolves toward the narrow end of the island. When the wolves reached the end, they either had to fight the stags or leave the island. The wolves decided to jump into the water and swim toward the mainland, which they reached safely.

The rabbits and the deer now lived happily together. The number of deer increased and the number of rabbits increased. But as their populations increased, they ate more and more food.

Black-and-white drawing
From the cover of *Canadian Forum*, January 1928

Soon the deer had to eat every plant they could find, even the thorny ones. They became desperate for food. Some of the deer stood on their hind legs to eat the leaves and branches higher up on the trees, while others ate the coarse bark.

The rabbits still found enough small plants to eat. But the deer destroyed the low branches and bushes they needed to hide from their enemies. The hawks and owls could now find the rabbits quite easily.

A few years after the wolves had been chased off the island, most of the trees were dying or dead. Only a few rabbits remained, all of the deer were starving, and the hawks and the owls had flown away.

During the winter, a pack of wolves crossed the ice to visit the island. The wolves were still there when the ice melted in the spring. Soon the trees began to grow again, the number of deer and rabbits increased, and the hawks and owls returned.

Black-and-white drawing and stainless steel etching (circa 1952)
Advertisements for Atlas Steels Limited, Welland, Ontario

THE SMART ONES

A PAIR OF CANOEISTS paddled their craft close to the lake shore and pulled the canoe onto the beach. They strolled beside the lake for awhile, and then walked into the forest. It was a beautiful day. As they walked, they talked and photographed the plants and animals.

Later, the pair stopped in a small clearing to rest. It was soon time to return to their canoe. Entering the forest again, they found a deer trail and followed it. It seemed to curve in the wrong direction, so they veered off the trail until they reached a clearing among the trees. It was the same clearing they had visited an hour before. They were lost!

The canoeists turned around slowly, wondering which direction to take. They saw several animals watching them. A white-tailed deer stood beside a beech tree, a red squirrel chattered in a sugar maple, and a blue jay sang from a yellow birch. After looking at each one, the people said, "Dumb animals. They cannot communicate with us."

Three mallard ducks flew low overhead. The people saw the ducks set their wings to land and then heard a splash. They ran toward the noise, rushing through a narrow strip of black spruce.

They found the lake, but their sudden arrival frightened the ducks away. The canoeists were disappointed that the birds were leaving. Nevertheless, they called their thanks to the mallards for indicating the way back to the canoe.

The mallards quacked, "Dumb animals. They cannot communicate with us."

Thoreau MacDonald's personal bookplate (undated)
From the Thoreau MacDonald Papers, Thomas Fisher Rare Book
Library, University of Toronto

CHEER UP, CHEER UP

A LARGE MAPLE TREE GREW on a hill in the centre of the city. Walking toward the tree, a woman exclaimed, "Finally, city council has given us permission to build a high-rise tower, right here on top of Clover Hill!"

A robin watched from her nest on a low branch of the tree. She called, "This is university land. It's the last piece of green space in the centre of the city. How did you get permission to build here?"

"The university doesn't have enough money to pay its teachers and do research. It had to sell some of its land and we bought it," the woman answered.

"Why do you want this land?" asked the robin.

"A group of us bought it as a financial investment," the woman replied. "We will make money from renting space in the new building. The university will earn money from the sale of the land. The city will collect more taxes. Everyone benefits from economic development."

"When will you start?" inquired the robin.

"We'll cut down your tree tomorrow, and start digging...."

"Cut down my tree! Tomorrow! You can't start tomorrow! You can't cut down my tree!" the robin chirped in panic. "I need another day to hatch my eggs, and fourteen days before the nestlings leave. You can't start for fifteen more days!"

"We must not deprive the people of the benefits of development," the woman explained. "Your tree must be removed so an attractive high-rise tower can grow and prosper in its place."

"Trees provide shade – they help to cool the city in summertime," the robin cried.

"We will air-condition the entire building," said the woman.

"Trees are beautiful," the robin pleaded.

"We'll add as many trees as necessary, in colourful plastic pots," the woman replied.

"You don't understand," the robin said frantically. "Trees are valuable!"

"There is nothing more valuable than high-rise buildings! I know. I am a businesswoman!" came the sharp reply.

The robin then asked, "What do you know about the value of wild animals and plants in the city, like robins or maple trees?"

"Not very much," the woman admitted.

"Perhaps you should learn more about ecology – about how different species interact with their environment," suggested the robin. "Climb up here. Study my nest. Count my eggs. Admire their exquisite colour. Watch how I protect them from predators."

The woman climbed to where the robin was sitting.

"Climb a little higher, so you can look into my nest," the robin coaxed as she flew off her nest.

The woman climbed higher to inspect the nest below. "Your nest is fascinating in design. There are four lovely eggs. They are a beautiful blue colour. But you were unwise to build here – your eggs will be broken tomorrow."

The robin was enraged by these words. She attacked the woman, pecking at her nose and eyes. The woman was startled and lost hold of the tree. She fell headfirst to the ground.

The leaves and twigs on the earth beneath the tree cushioned her fall. "I am not hurt," said the woman, looking up at the robin, "and I can't blame you. I would have done exactly what you did. Humans and birds are similar, in many ways."

The woman got up and limped away, but she returned each day to watch the robin and her nest. On the fifteenth day, she was thrilled to watch the four young robins take their first flight. Soon after, the birds migrated south for the winter.

Next spring, three of the young robins returned. Instead of seeing a high-rise tower, they found a beautiful garden with a large birdbath under the maple tree. It was sculpted in the shape of a robin, from a rough piece of red and black granite.

"Cheer up, cheer up," sang the robins, as they splashed happily in the birdbath.

Black-and-white drawing
From *Birds & Animals, 2nd Series* (1973),
Thoreau MacDonald, privately published

THE TASTE TEST

O NE MORNING AFTER A LATE SUMMER RAIN, thousands of white mushrooms suddenly appeared on the forest floor. Since most of the deer mice in the forest had never seen mushrooms before, they eagerly gathered to study them. At the front of the group a young mouse and an old mouse stood side by side.

"What are these? Are they good to eat?" the young mouse asked.

"They're called mushrooms. Some mushrooms are good and some are poisonous," the old mouse replied.

"Are these good?"

"Some mice died from eating mushrooms last year, but I don't know which kind they ate," said the old mouse.

The young mouse moved over to sniff a mushroom. "This one smells very sweet," he said. "It must be good to eat."

"Look!" squeaked another mouse. "That squirrel is eating the mushrooms."

All of the mice turned to watch the squirrel.

The young mouse looked up at the old mouse. "The squirrel is eating the mushrooms, so they must be good," he said.

"Not necessarily," replied the old mouse. "The squirrel might die later, or the poison in the mushrooms might not hurt squirrels."

"Then how do I decide if it's safe to eat them?" pressured the young mouse.

The old mouse looked thoughtful. "Well, you could start by eating just a little bit or you could not eat any until they are proven safe to eat."

"What will you do?" the young mouse asked of his elder.

"I will not eat any," answered the old mouse.

The majority of the mice decided to eat the sweet-smelling mushrooms. A few others, including the old mouse and his young friend, decided not to eat the mushrooms until they were proven safe to eat.

The mushrooms were truly delicious. But they were also poisonous. All of the mice who ate the beautiful white mushrooms died.

The remaining deer mice and white mushrooms lived on.

Black-and-white linoleum cut
From *Canadian Forum* February (1922)
[This is the first published work of Thoreau MacDonald]

THE ACORN AND THE OAK TREE

A RED SQUIRREL SCAMPERED among the branches of a large white oak tree, chewing off acorns for her winter store. One acorn fell to the ground and settled beside a rotting log.

"I believe a tree could live here forever," the acorn said. "Next spring I will sprout into an oak tree. I will produce many acorns."

The next spring, the acorn sprouted into an oak tree. Rooted in fertile soil beside a large lake, it grew quickly. Tall oak and pine trees growing nearby sheltered the young oak from strong winds. Plenty of sunlight reached the tree's leaves.

"I am very lucky," it said. "I will soon become a big tree and produce many acorns."

Every year Native people came to the forest to gather acorns. They soaked the acorns to remove the bitter taste, and then dried them for making soup and bread. Harvest time was a happy time. The young oak tree enjoyed these visits.

Then people came with axes to harvest the trees to build houses and factories. All of the large trees were removed, except the oak and pine. Standing tall and straight, the young oak tree was proud to know the people were saving the oak and pine to build ships for the Royal Navy.

Years passed and the settlers followed the loggers. They cut or burned almost all the trees, to convert the forest into fields. They wanted to grow corn, beans, squash and potatoes instead of trees. The oak tree survived because the land where it grew was too rocky to farm.

The tree grew tall and stately. As it looked across the open landscape, it felt sad. After many years of logging, the forest was almost all gone. Wistfully, the white oak thought, "I will soon be cut, too. I cannot live forever but I may last forever – as a sturdy stable floor or as a stout barn door."

With most of the forest gone, the winds grew stronger and began to blow the soil off the fields. Drifting soil covered roads and crops, and sometimes the sky turned yellow. People planted trees along roads to stop the soil from drifting and the oak tree was pleased when they planted some of its acorns. But not enough trees were planted, and the soil continued to erode.

More people became alarmed. Then someone suggested creating a park to save the remaining plants and animals in the region. The oak tree was overjoyed. "No one will cut me now," it said. "I will produce acorns forever!"

A trail that led to the white oak became popular for hiking. At first, this pleased the tree greatly. But thousands of feet packed the soil and injured the tree's roots. Some people carved their names deeply into its bark.

Then a dam was built to raise the water level in the lake so larger ships could pass by, and the great oak's roots were flooded during the growing season. This deprived them of oxygen and the tree began to die.

Air pollution from cars, trucks, airplanes, factories, stores, office buildings and houses increased to a level that began to poison the plants and animals. The failing oak now suffered from injury to its leaves and damage to its roots.

The great oak tree lived for 300 years and died in three. In its final year, it produced a tremendous crop of acorns. Each acorn promised to grow into a tree to replace the great white oak. But all of the acorns fell into the water, except one that was caught in a fork of the tree.

When a strong autumn wind blew down the dead oak tree, the

acorn that was caught in the fork rolled free and landed on a small island. "I believe a tree could live here forever," it said. "Next spring I will sprout into an oak tree. I will produce many acorns."

Black-and-white drawing
From *Birds & Animals* (1968), Thoreau MacDonald,
privately printed

HAWK HAVEN

Two farmers were chatting over the fence that separated their properties.

Only two trees grew on the farm to the east. This farmer bragged about his fine grain crop. He also complained of the large number of mice that were eating the grain before it was ripe enough to harvest.

Many trees grew along the fencerows and laneways of the other farm. This farmer also bragged about his grain crop, but explained he had very few mice.

As the farmers chatted, a red-tailed hawk landed in a nearby maple tree. It perched on a branch, searching for mice in the field below. The hawk soon saw a mouse, swooped down, caught it and flew up to perch in a cherry tree to eat it. Then the hawk flew to a pine tree to rest and preen its feathers.

The two farmers parted. As they walked back to their barns, one blessed and the other cursed his luck. Above the trees, the hawk circled as it watched the field below for mice.

V-FORMATION
[Dedicated to the Innu of Labrador]

Ｏne day an elder Canada goose announced that she would lead a flock of geese on a low-level flight over the forest. At sunrise the next morning, more than a thousand geese gathered on the wide bay at the mouth of the river.

The elder goose spread her wings and honked loudly as she rose up and circled over the bay. Then, with the other Canada geese following, she flew up the full length of the river valley and back again.

All the geese honked loudly as they followed the leader. flying side-by-side in a large group was much more fun than flying in small groups, as they had done until now. And it thrilled them to skim closely over the tree tops.

The number of geese joining these flights grew larger each day. Soon the flock blotted out the sun as it flew over the forest. The plants and soil in the river valley turned white from goose droppings. The deafening honks and thunderous wing-beats of thousands of low-flying geese frightened the animals below.

So alarmed were the forest animals by these low-level flights that young caribou fled from the herd in terror. Young chickadees crashed into trees in panic. Many other animals slipped and fell in goose droppings. Even the great horned owl, asleep on the branch of a black spruce tree, was startled into flight only to be showered by the offensive droppings.

Angry and hurt, the animals assembled before the great horned owl, who was widely known as a wise bird. Surely she could help them settle their dispute with the Canada geese.

The caribou described how their young were being separated

from their mothers, and the chickadees told how their young were injured every day in collisions. They all wanted the geese to stop flying so low over the forest.

The geese claimed that their flights disturbed only a few forest animals for only a few minutes each day. They proposed adding two new flight paths, including one out to sea, so the disturbance from their flights would be even less.

All the forest animals watched the great horned owl as she announced her verdict. She hooted loudly, "It would be unfair to tell the Canada geese that they must stop flying low, but we must be certain that they understand how low-level flights endanger the other animals. My ruling is this: every species deserves respect. Each time the geese make a low flight over other animals, they must fly just as low over their goose nests, too."

All of the geese began honking in alarm. The elder goose interrupted them with a furious flapping of wings. "We must not harm our goslings," she said. Then she led the flock away.

The next morning, there were so many geese swimming on the bay that the water was black and white with feathers. The elder goose honked loudly as she took off, circled over the bay and flew higher and higher. All of the geese followed. As they flew high over the goose nests, they spread into a V-shape that was so wide it spanned three river valleys.

Hearing faint honking, the forest animals turned to watch the flock pass high above. The great horned owl looked on from the top of a tamarack tree. She hooted in respect as the geese flew over. They flew so high and so wide apart that not a single owl feather was spattered white with droppings.

CONCRETE THINKING

Each spring the frogs lay their eggs in swamp water. As the water warms, the eggs hatch into tadpoles that develop into young frogs.

Frogs know they must migrate away from the swamp where they were born to find enough food to eat. They may migrate as far as two kilometres from the swamp before they return to breed.

It used to be easy for the frogs to hop through the forest and across open areas. Now they often have to cross highways where they may be injured or killed by the fast moving cars and trucks.

One spring, a young pickerel frog began to migrate back to his swamp to breed. He hopped safely across a highway until he came to a solid concrete wall. He joined thousands of amphibians and reptiles trying to get over the wall. It was impossible.

A flock of crows perched on top of the wall to watch the struggling frogs. The young frog asked the nearest crow: "Is there a hole in the wall that I can pass through?"

"It's a solid wall, as far as I can see," replied the crow.

"Why is the wall here?" asked the frog.

"It keeps the cars and trucks that are going one way from hitting the cars and trucks going the other way," said the crow.

"The wall doesn't have to be solid to do that," insisted the frog. "It could have holes in it that would let the animals through."

"The wall is designed to save human lives and not the lives of mere frogs and other small animals," cawed the crow.

"This wall is poorly designed. It will kill more people than before," claimed the frog, while trying to jump over the wall again.

Back-and-white drawing
Cover design for the Spring 1945 Catalogue of Ryerson Books,
Ryerson Press, Toronto

"Impossible. It is just a concrete wall," argued the crow.

"Wait and see," said the frog. "The wall is blocking our migration corridor. We don't know which way to turn. The traffic is killing us and the road is becoming slippery. There will soon be a human accident."

A few minutes later, a car spun out of control, a truck jackknifed, and over 100 cars and trucks smashed into each other. Dozens of people were killed and many more were injured.

The accident broke some holes through the concrete wall, which were large enough for the small animals to cross to the other side. As the animals ran, hopped, slithered and crawled around and over the wrecked vehicles, government officials rushed to the scene.

Later the officials announced, "The accident was caused by thousands of tiny frogs trying to hop across the highway. They have turned the highway into a slippery mess. We cannot tolerate another accident like this. A concrete wall will be built around the swamp so the frogs will not be able to leave the water. There is no other option."

The young pickerel frog hopped through a hole in the wall to join his friends in the swamp.

Black-and-white drawing
From *David and Other Poems* (1942), Earle Birney,
Ryerson Press, Toronto

MOUNTAIN KING

A TROPHY HUNTER SPENT three months searching for the largest bighorn sheep on the mountain. Finally, he found it, standing on a ledge above the hunter. Its magnificent horns were silhouetted against the snow-capped mountain.

The bighorn sheep saw the hunter and backed into a crevice where it was no longer visible. The hunter raised his rifle, adjusted the telescopic sight and waited for a good shot.

The bighorn sheep did not move.

"Come out. You are wasting my time. I am the true king of the mountain," the hunter shouted to the bighorn sheep. At the same time, he fired a shot at the mountain to frighten the animal.

The noise of the hunter's voice and the rifle shot echoed through the mountain. The mountain replied. A low rumble swelled into a roar as an avalanche tumbled down the slope. It swept beside the bighorn sheep and over the hunter.

Black-and-white drawing
From *A Canadian Child's ABC* (1931), Ronald K. Gordon and
Thoreau MacDonald, Dent, Toronto and Vancouver;
and from *A Canadian ABC* (1990), Lyn Cook, drawings by
Thoreau MacDonald, Penumbra Press, Waterloo, Ontario

THE LIFELINE

A FATHER BUILT A WOODEN TRAIN for his son. He carved the engine and nine passenger cars from blocks of white pine. Sugar maple pegs were shaped into people. Ten stations were carved from white birch.

"Made in Canada, from Canadian wood products," the father said proudly. "Let's call it *The Canadian*."

"What will you name the stations?" asked the boy.

"That is your choice," his father replied. "Whatever you want."

The boy was pleased with his new toy. First, he set up stations at Halifax, Moncton, Saint John, Montreal, Ottawa, Sudbury, Winnipeg, Regina, Kicking Horse and Vancouver. Then he placed ten people in front of each station, except Vancouver, the last stop on the line. He also placed some pictures between the stations to show the view from the train's windows.

The boy started the train at Halifax. It picked up all the people standing at the stations and delivered 90 people to Vancouver. He then turned the train around, picked up all the people and returned them home.

"Maybe," the boy said, "*The Canadian* will travel faster if I rearrange the people." So he moved some people west, leaving two at Halifax, four at Moncton, six at Saint John, increasing by two each time, until Kicking Horse. But the train took just as long to pick up the 90 passengers and deliver them to Vancouver.

"Now I'll close a station," he thought, choosing Halifax. The train started at Moncton this time, so it made a faster trip to Vancouver. But two people were left standing at Halifax.

He closed Moncton next, then Saint John, and then Montreal. "Each time I close a station, my train makes a faster trip," he said.

"Saving time saves money, so I will close the first four stations on the line. Only 20 people will be left standing, and I will be the owner of a richer train company!"

"If you do that," his father said, "how will the people left standing at the stations visit their friends in Ottawa or Vancouver?"

"Some other way," said the boy.

"They and their friends will be unhappy," his father replied.

The boy paused to think. He set up his train at Vancouver, with all nine cars attached. "You're right, Dad. I've just figured out that if I hurt one end of the line, I hurt the other end, too. The end of the line is the beginning!" exclaimed the boy triumphantly.

Just then the boy's sister entered the room, obviously upset. "Have you heard about acid rain? It can kill dragonflies, leopard frogs, lake trout and sugar maple trees, and that hurts us, too!"

Her brother looked puzzled. The girl kneeled beside the train and rearranged the stations in a circle, "Look," she said. "This station is Insects. This one's Frogs. Then Fish, Trees and Humans. Now let's see what happens when we close some of them."

Black-and-white linoleum cut
From *The Circle of Affection* (1947), Duncan Campbell Scott, McClelland and Stewart, Toronto

WILDERNESS

A LOON WAS ENJOYING A LEISURELY SWIM in a large lake. The sun warmed her back as she watched a light rain begin to fall in the distance.

A rainbow appeared in the sky.

"I have heard there is a treasure at the end of the rainbow," said the loon to herself. "I wonder which end of the rainbow holds the treasure."

The loon decided to fly toward the rainbow to search for the treasure. As she flew up, she noticed the ends of the rainbow grew longer. She flew higher and higher, and the rainbow grew longer and longer, until it became a complete ring.

"Where is the treasure now?" she wondered.

The loon looked through the rain ring. She saw her lake and the forest below.

"I see it now," she laughed loudly for all to hear. "The rain ring surrounds the treasure!"

Black-and-white drawing
From *Thoreau MacDonald: Illustrator, Designer, Observer of Nature* (1971), L. Bruce Pierce, Norflex Limited, Toronto

TWO HABITATS

While keeping watch one day, a hoary marmot saw a gray wolf climbing up the mountain toward the alpine meadow where the marmots lived. The marmot whistled a warning and all of its friends in the colony scampered safely into their burrows dug among the rocks.

The wolf walked into the marmot colony. He stopped at a burrow, sniffed to be sure there was a marmot inside and began to dig. He was hungry for marmot.

The marmot poked up her head from another burrow to ask, "Why are you digging here? You can't catch us by digging. All of our passageways are connected."

"I am digging a wolf den," pretended the wolf as he continued to dig. "This is a beautiful place to raise my family."

"Dig on," chuckled the marmot, for she knew the soil was too shallow to build a den deep enough for wolves.

The wolf kept digging, but each hole he dug was blocked by boulders. Finally, he sat back on his haunches to rest his sore paws. "It is impossible to build a den here," said the frustrated wolf. "I would freeze in wintertime. How can you possibly live in such a barren place?"

"We like it," replied the marmot from a safe distance. "We have a magnificent view. When we see our predators coming toward us, we have time to hide in our burrows. Our burrows are safe among the rocks, and the alpine vegetation is delicious."

The wolf shivered. "There is nothing here that appeals to me," he said.

The marmots watched the wolf leave their colony. He walked down the mountain and disappeared into the forest. Later, when the marmots heard wolves howling in the forest below, they chuckled and continued to frolic on their alpine meadow.

Black-and-white drawing
From the cover of *Canadian Forum*, February 1928

THE HAWK AND THE CHICKADEE

A HAWK SPIED A CHICKADEE flying through the forest and decided to catch her. "The chickadee will be surprised," he said to himself.

The black-capped chickadee saw the hawk coming and closed her wings. She fell like a stone. The sharp-shinned hawk expected this reaction and adjusted his angle downward.

The chickadee opened her wings again and flew alongside the largest branch of a red maple tree. "The hawk will be surprised," she called to her friends in the forest.

As the hawk prepared to snatch the chickadee, he saw that he would crash into the branch and be hurt. The hawk soared upward instead and the chickadee landed to eat some seeds.

Black and white drawing
From the cover of the 1967 Annual Meeting, Thoreau Society,
Concord, Massachusetts

THE HYBRIDS

A BEAUTIFUL EASTERN WHITE PINE TREE grew on the edge of a great forest. It was tall and straight with long, thin needles that felt feathery to touch. The tree was so beautiful that some people decided to harvest its cones, extract the seeds and grow new trees just like it.

"I wonder if we could make this beautiful tree even better," one person asked. Others agreed to try.

They searched far and wide until they found another lovely tree. They collected some pollen from this tree and dusted it on the cones of the beautiful pine tree. When the cones matured two years later, the seeds were planted in an area that had been recently logged. It soon became obvious that these trees, with two parents located far apart, grew more quickly than the trees that had local parents.

The improved trees appeared superior to the others. They grew much faster and were more beautiful. The difference in growth rate was remarkable. The tree planters soon demanded only the improved trees. From then on, the slower-growing pine trees were seldom planted.

One summer, after the first forest planted with improved trees was forty years old, there was a very long period without rain. The needles wilted on all the pine trees. The tops of many of the fastest growing trees died. The improved trees were no longer so beautiful.

During the dry period, a major epidemic of pine bark beetles occurred. The beetles bored beneath the bark of all of the pine trees and laid their eggs.

The local pines were able to flood the insect holes with resin which killed the eggs. The improved trees were unable to do so and the hatching insects killed the trees instead.

A forest inspector came to see how the planted trees were doing and was very disappointed. "Improved trees are not proven trees," he said. "In this case, they did not produce enough resin to protect themselves."

Later that season, cones from the local pine trees were gathered to extract the seed and grow new trees just like them.

Black-and-white drawing
From *Canadian Forum,* March 1930

THE PLOUGHERS

A HORSE STOPPED PULLING THE PLOUGH, turned its head to look at the farmer and said, "It is your turn to pull."

The farmer responded by flicking the reins against the horse's rump.

The horse refused to move.

The farmer flicked the reins harder and commanded: "Slave, obey your master."

"I am not your slave. I am your equal," the horse said defiantly.

"Why do you think you are equal to me?" laughed the farmer.

"Because we are both animals, and because we both need and help each other," the horse replied.

"Perhaps you are superior – you always walk ahead of me," the farmer joked, and flicked the reins once more.

The horse remained still.

"Please pull the plough, my good friend," the farmer pleaded.

"Master and slave are never friends," the horse replied.

"In truth, you are my best friend," the farmer admitted. "Let me help you pull."

The horse leaned into its collar and began to pull again as the farmer guided the plough.

Black-and-white drawing
From *Talks With a Hunter* (1946), Thoreau MacDonald,
privately published

THE WINTERBERRY SHRUB

A WINTERBERRY SHRUB STOOD ON THE EDGE of a large tamarack bog. As its leaves grew in springtime, small greenish-white flowers appeared on the shrub.

The bees and other insects visited the winterberry flowers to obtain nectar. When they visited a male flower, they picked up some pollen. When they visited a female flower, they deposited some of the pollen, which would fertilize the flower.

By late summer, each fertilized flower had developed into a brilliant red fruit the size of a pea. The shrub was magnificent in colour. It said to itself, "I am the most beautiful one in the bog. The other plants and animals are quite drab in comparison. The bog would be much nicer without them."

Recalling that its life had begun when a blue jay dropped a nutlet by the edge of the bog where the shrub now grew, the winterberry shrub decided it was proper for blue jays to stay in the bog – but no others.

Then the shrub remembered that other fruit-eating birds spread winterberry nutlets, too. Perhaps it was alright for all of the fruit-eating birds to live in the bog – but no one else.

The previous year the shrub had nearly been killed by insects that ate many of its leaves, until some insect-eating birds saved its life. Fruit-eating and insect-eating birds would be allowed to stay – but no one else.

A month before, a mouse had begun to eat the shrub's bark, until a marsh hawk caught the mouse and saved the plant. Now the winterberry shrub decided it wanted all of the birds to remain – but no one else.

Just then a bee flew by and landed on the bluish-purple flower of a bog aster. The bee looked like those who had fertilized the shrub's flowers three months before. The little winterberry shrub felt warm as the sun shone on its bright red berries. It now welcomed all the birds, insects and plants living in the bog.

Black-and-white drawings
From *Birds and Animals* (1971), second series,
Thoreau MacDonald, privately published

THE WOLF HUNT

A moose watched in amazement as two people hunted a wolf from a helicopter. They kept shooting at the wolf as it dodged from tree to tree, searching frantically for a place to hide.

"Why are they shooting at you from a helicopter?" called the moose. "It must be a terrifying experience. There is no chance to escape!"

"The politician in charge of wild animals has ordered as many wolves killed as possible because sometimes we kill moose," wailed the wolf.

"What an excellent idea! It is rare to find such a wise person," the moose replied.

"You don't understand," howled the wolf. "The plan is to grow more moose, so more moose hunters will be happy."

"That's wrong! Hide under my belly," shouted the moose, as the helicopter flew into position for another shot. "They will not shoot at me. The moose hunting season has not started yet."

"You have saved my life," said the panting wolf. "But why did you do it? My sharp teeth are close to your throat."

The moose watched the helicopter fly out of sight. Then he leapt aside, turned to face the wolf, lowered his antlers and replied: "We who live in the wilderness learn to respect each other."

Black-and-white drawing
From *The Iceberg and Other Poems* (1934),
Charles G.D. Roberts, Ryerson Press, Toronto

POLAR BEAR REFLECTIONS

A POLAR BEAR CLIMBED OUT OF THE WATER onto a melting iceberg. Looking down, the bear saw his reflection in a shallow pool that had formed on top of the ice.

At first, he thought there was another bear under the ice. Soon he realized he was looking at his own reflection.

The bear walked into the pool and stood still. He enjoyed watching himself. He put his head down and touched the image with his nose. This created a small wave. The wave spread and distorted the bear's reflection, which made the bear angry. He pawed at the water. This made more waves and his reflection disappeared.

The bear stood up on his hind feet and growled at the ocean, ice and clouds. As he growled, the water in the pool became still and the bear saw his reflection again. This time he saw an angry bear.

As the puzzled bear peered at himself and the moving reflection of ice and clouds, a light breeze rippled the water in the pool and distorted the picture. The wind grew stronger and the reflection of the white bear in its habitat disappeared.

"Everything in my world is in motion," said the polar bear as it turned to face the wind.

"Everything in the world is in motion," whistled the wind.

Black-and-white drawing
From *Abitibi Adventure* (1950), Jack Hambleton,
Longmans, Green and Company, Toronto

LOON LAUGHTER

Common loons have three different songs – an eerie wail, a warning or distress call and a yodelling laugh. A young naturalist became very worried about a pair of adult loons and a baby loon on her lake, for they never laughed.

Each spring the acidic pollutants that had accumulated in the snow and ice over winter were suddenly released into the lake. They killed the young fish. The old fish lived on but they were too big for a baby loon to eat.

The naturalist considered catching the baby and feeding it. Then she decided to buy some small fish from the fish hatchery to give to the loon parents to feed the young one.

The naturalist bought a barrel full of young speckled trout and rowed out to meet the loons at the end of the lake. As the boat approached, the loons began to sing their distress song. Too weak to swim any longer, the baby rode on its mother's back.

Trying not to frighten the loons, the naturalist rowed closer and carefully ladled a few fish into the water. The father loon became ecstatic when he saw the first trout. He dove immediately and chased the fish relentlessly, using foot and wing strokes to change direction as the fish darted from side to side.

The loon soon caught the fish and surfaced with a splash. He joyfully presented it to the baby, as the mother turned to watch.

The baby ate the fish slowly, gaining strength with each mouthful. Suddenly, the young loon was tossed into the water as its mother dove to chase another fish.

She caught the fish and fed it to the baby loon. Then she began to yodel. Her mate joined her and their laughter echoed through the hills.

Black-and-white drawing
From *Indian Nights* (1930), Isabel Ecclestone Mackay,
McClelland & Stewart, Toronto

SALMON PARK

Each year the Atlantic salmon swam upstream to lay and fertilize their eggs in a beautiful gravel-bottomed pool. The clear, rippling water was home to the young salmon before they moved downstream to the sea.

Bears and eagles visited the pool to feed on the salmon. People came too, to spear, net and fish all the salmon they could catch.

Eventually, some of the people decided to live beside the pool so they could be close to their favourite fishing area all the time.

After many years of settlement, a town grew up around the pool. Careful to protect the precious salmon, the new generation of townspeople reserved the pool area as a park, and forbade further fishing in the pool. A bridge was built across the stream that flowed from the pool and people often walked onto the bridge to watch and admire the large fish swimming below.

When the town was small, the rainwater flowed slowly into the salmon pool. As the town grew larger, the rainwater that fell on roofs, roads and parking lots flowed faster over the pavement to storm sewers and into the pool. The sudden surges of water washed the salmon eggs downstream where they were covered with silt and died.

Eventually, the salmon no longer returned to the pool. People still walk across the bridge, hoping to see the salmon. They look down at the clear, rippling water in the gravel-bottomed pool, but the salmon have disappeared.

Black-and-white drawing
From *Hurt Not the Earth* (1958), E. Newton-White,
Ryerson Press, Toronto

SURVIVAL

Smelling smoke, a red squirrel climbed to the top of a tall tree to look around. He ran down quickly, calling as loudly as he could, "Fire! Fire! The forest is on fire! Run for your lives!"

As a white-tailed deer ran by, the squirrel leapt onto her back. "Please carry me to the lake," he pleaded. "I'm not a fast runner, but I want to live, too."

"Survival of the fittest means survival of the fastest," said the deer. "Hold on to me and you will be safe". Unfortunately, the deer ran close to a white spruce tree whose branches swept the squirrel onto the ground.

A black bear ran by and the squirrel jumped onto his back. "Please carry me to the lake," he pleaded. "I'm not a strong runner, but I want to live, too."

"Survival of the fittest means survival of the strongest," said the bear. "Hold on to me and you will be safe." Then he reared onto his hind legs to see which way to go. The squirrel fell to the ground as the bear ran off.

Looking around dizzily, the squirrel realized that he could not depend on others. He would have to save himself. But how?

Suddenly, the deer and the bear reappeared.

"Why did you come back?" the squirrel asked.

"The wind is blowing hard. It blew burning embers over our heads and set fire to the forest in front of us. We are surrounded by fire! What can we do?" the deer and bear cried in alarm.

"Survival of the fittest means adapting to change," said the squirrel. "Bear, run to your den in the cliff and dig deeper. The fire will not be fierce among the rocks. Deer, run into the centre of that swamp and lie down, with just your nose above water."

"What will you do?" asked the bear. "Jump on my back and come with me."

"Come with me," said the deer.

"Thank you, but don't worry," replied the squirrel confidently. "I'll survive in my own way."

As the others ran off, the squirrel ran toward a white pine tree. The pine was the oldest and largest tree in the forest. It had survived seven fires, because its bark was too thick to burn through during the brief time the fire passed by.

The squirrel had often climbed this tree to chew off pine cones and eat the seeds. He remembered that near the top of the tree, a broken branch stub had rotted away to form a deep cavity. The squirrel scampered up the tree and crawled inside.

Though the fire passed beneath it, the squirrel was high enough to be safe. The deer and the bear survived, and the thick bark saved the life of the tree.

Black-and-white drawing
From "Notes for Maria Chapdelaine," *Thoreau MacDonald's Notebooks* (1980), Penumbra Press, Moonbeam, Ontario

THE SNAKE AND THE CYCLIST

A snake was sunning herself on a path through the forest where the sun shone warmly between the trees.

Suddenly, the snake saw a person on a bicycle racing towards her. The snake tried to slither off the trail but she was not fast enough and the bicycle ran over the tip of her tail.

"Ouch!" cried the snake. "You crushed my tail!"

"I'm sorry. I thought you were just a stick lying on the path," apologized the cyclist. "Why are you lying on the trail?"

"This is my forest," said the snake. "I can go wherever I please. Why are you riding a bicycle through my forest?"

"This is a national park," replied the cyclist. "People walk or cycle on the trails here. In fact, the park managers built this bicycle trail so more people would study the wildlife."

"Do you think that was a good idea? What have you learned about snakes from the seat of your bicycle?" scolded the snake.

The cyclist hesitated, embarrassed, and then said: "Are you a milk snake? You are beautiful."

"Yes, I am, thank you," replied the snake. "I am the only female milk snake left in the park."

The snake slithered slowly into the forest. The cyclist walked slowly along the nature trail.

Black-and-white drawing
From the cover of *Canadian Forum*, May 1927

THE TRILLIUMS AND THE BEAR

A YOUNG BLACK BEAR EMERGED SLEEPILY from the den where he had hibernated through the winter. He was very hungry.

A few weeks later, after crossing woods and meadows, he found himself in a large and beautiful patch of white trilliums. Their smooth, creamy-white petals were so tempting that he tasted one of the flowers. It was delicious! There were a few red trilliums, too, which he liked just as much. Greedily, the bear gorged himself on the trilliums.

"You should eat no more than one plant in ten," said the trilliums. "If you take more, you will gradually kill us."

"I have eaten much more than that already," said the bear, and continued to eat. "That is the price you must pay for being so delicious."

The next spring the bear ate more trilliums.

"You are eating us too quickly," warned the trilliums. "We cannot reproduce fast enough. Our numbers are falling."

"I still see lots of tasty trilliums, so I'll eat as many of you as I want," replied the bear.

The next spring the trilliums were much fewer in number. There were not enough to fatten the bear.

"You are truly magnificent flowers, but you have disappointed me," said the bear to the trilliums. "I have depended on you for food each spring. Now you have failed me and I am very hungry."

The trilliums replied sadly, "That is the price you must pay for eating too many of us."

Black-and-white drawing
From *Woods and Fields* (1951), Thoreau MacDonald,
Ryerson Press, Toronto

CARIBOU CROSSING

A HERD OF WOODLAND CARIBOU was migrating toward the calving ground where the young would be born. The caribou grazed on birch twigs and lichen as they followed a trail that had been used for centuries.

As the caribou curved down a gentle slope to cross the river, they found it overflowing its banks. This was unusual because the snow was still deep among the spruce trees.

The leaders of the caribou herd walked round and round, unwilling to enter the fast-flowing stream. Though they had crossed the river at this place many times, none had ever seen the water this high. Finally, one of the leaders walked into the river and the rest followed.

More than a thousand caribou entered the river but only the strongest reached the other side. The rest were pushed downstream by the violent current.

The speed of the current swept the caribou into a narrow stretch of rapids. Many of the animals were dashed against the rocks and drowned. A few passed through the rapids unharmed and were able to swim across the stream. A day later, six canoeists paddled by the caribou crossing. They took photographs of the hundreds of dead and dying caribou lining the shore.

The disaster became an international story and the government ordered an investigation. It showed that a new hydroelectric dam that had been built upstream caused the tragedy. It examined whether the head of the hydroelectric company, the person who had opened the floodgate to generate more electricity, or the customers who wanted more and more electricity were to blame.

Finally, the investigators decided it was the caribou who were at fault. "The wild animals must change their way of life to co-exist with humans. The fittest caribou will survive."

Soon after the announcement, the earth began to quake. The immense weight of the water held behind the dam had pressed down and twisted the land. The dam cracked, then collapsed. A tremendous surge of water flowed down the valley and the river returned to normal.

TADDLE POND

A DIVERSE COMMUNITY OF PLANTS and animals lived in a small pond in the middle of a huge city. On sunny days, the animals often relaxed side by side on a large cedar log that was partly submerged in the pond.

The log was the meeting place where the elder turtles, muskrats, beaver and other animals taught their young ones. Because all of the animals shared the same log, the young of each species learned from the elders of all species.

One day, the elder turtles decided they should control the log and the water surrounding it. They drew a boundary line on the water, which only they could see. Then they defended their territory so fiercely that the other animals had to move to another log.

Some of the young turtles objected when the other animals were forced to move away. They complained the elder turtles were ruining the community life in the pond, by becoming too rigid and narrow-minded.

A few of the young turtles decided to broaden their knowledge of the pond. Sometimes they left the turtle log to listen to the muskrats, beaver and other animals. This made the elder turtles very angry. They said only turtles could teach turtles. They claimed the elder turtles could teach the young turtles everything they needed to know.

Most of the young turtles were afraid to swim far from the turtle log. They had to obey or face punishment. But a few were determined to swim farther and to learn about the other organisms in and around the pond.

One day a young spotted turtle appeared before his elders.

Black-and-white drawing
from *Woods and Fields* (1951), Thoreau MacDonald,
Ryerson Press, Toronto

"I respectfully request permission to attend a lecture offered by the muskrats on the diversity of water plants in our pond," he said. "I want to learn how the muskrats create and maintain openings among water plants for turtles and ducks to use."

"Permission denied," decreed the elder turtles.

"Why?" asked the young turtle. "The young muskrats and beaver are free to go to any lecture. Why can't I?"

"Permission denied," the elder turtles repeated, snapping their mouths shut.

The young turtle shocked its elders when he spoke again. "I also request permission to attend a series of lectures offered by the beaver on the history of changes in the water level in our p..."

"Permission denied," interrupted the elders.

The young turtle replied in a calm, clear voice that was heard throughout the pond. "I must disobey your ruling. The students must make the final decision on which lectures to attend."

"Turtles who disobey must be expelled!" shouted a snapping turtle.

"Expelled!" chorused the elder turtles.

The young spotted turtle stretched his neck farther to address all of his friends in the pond. "I will always respect my elders. They have taught me the greatest lesson. The limits of one's mind define the limits of one's world."

Black-and-white brush drawing
From *Woods and Fields* (1951), Thoreau MacDonald,
Ryerson Press, Toronto

LOON LAUGHTER ACTIVITIES: A NATURE STUDY GUIDE
Celina Owen

The stories in *Loon Laughter* represent the real world. They present truths about human nature and about plant and animal behaviour.

The following activities are suggested ways of exploring some of the ideas expressed in this book. They challenge you to write, draw, discuss and think about animals, plants and people, and the relationships among them. Maybe you will discover something new through this exploration – about nature and about yourself.

1. Many traditional fables have a moral at the end that expresses the lesson the author intends the reader to learn from the story. For example, the moral of Aesop's well-known fable "The Tortoise and the Hare" is "Slow and steady wins the race." Each of the ecological fables in this book contains a moral even though it is not often expressed in writing. Identify the lesson of each ecological fable and then express it as a moral.

2. Try rewriting one of the ecological fables as though you were a plant, animal or person in the story. For example, you could rewrite "Caribou Crossing" from the point of view of a caribou, a photographer or an eagle nesting nearby. Consider what the character would observe. What details would be included in the story? What would be left out? What feelings would the character have about the happenings in the story?

3. Visit an area close to your home or school where plants and animals grow wild. Observe the ways in which human actions affect the lives of other organisms and the ways in which the actions of other organisms affect humans. Do gulls congregate at the park to feed on scraps left by people? Are tree branches damaged by fildren playing? Where do ants make their hills? Record your observations. Then try to explain them, or write a story using your observations as the basis for your explanation.

4. Some of these fables tell about ways people have changed the natural habitat in certain areas. Human activities cause the acid rain that hurts loons. Run-off from storm sewers kills salmon eggs. When too many trees are cut down, erosion and changes in wildlife habitat result. Choose an environmental problem that you would like to research. Consult books, magazine and newspaper articles, television documentaries and organizations that study the problem you are researching. Find out how the problem is caused and what is being done to improve the situation. Is there anything you can do to help?

5. Create an illustration in the style of Thoreau MacDonald. Thoreau primarily used pen or pencil on paper to create his unique line drawings. How will you create the effect that you see in his art? Note the way he drew the sky, and reflections on water. What features of his drawing will you mimic to make your creation resemble a Thoreau MacDonald creation?

6.a Which story in this book is most meaningful for you? Why? Write down everything that the story reminds you of (books, movies, things that have happened to you) and how it makes you feel when you read it. Can you explain why this story is more powerful for you than other stories? Why does it "stand out" for you? Will your life change in any way as a result of reading this story? Why or why not?

6.b Contrast the story that is most meaningful for you with those of other people. Ask each person to share the reasons why that particular story stands out for her or him. Why do different people like different stories?

7. The following passage is the beginning of an unpublished story. How would you finish it? When you have completed your story, ask yourself, "Is my story an ecological fable? Why or why not? Does it have a moral?"

A pileated woodpecker migrated north to build a nest in the pine forest where its great grandparents had lived. When it arrived, it was surprised to find only one pine tree still growing there.

8. Ask a friend or a group of people to sit comfortably with eyes closed while you read the following passage:

Imagine you are an animal or plant that lives in the forest. Your forest home fills all your needs: it provides you with food, water and shelter. Now your part of the forest is being cleared to build a hotel and resort complex. Harvesting machines and logging trucks rumble through the once-quiet forest. Trees crash to the earth and are hauled away. People bring portable shelters and construction equipment to begin work on the resort. Every day your habitat is disrupted more and more. Imagine ... what do you do? What do you think? How do you feel?

Consider how your thoughts, feelings and actions differ, depending on which organism you imagine yourself to be. What happens to you when you imagine yourself as a mature red pine tree? As a black bear cub? As a red fox? As a chickadee? As a pine bark beetle? How would you feel if you were a logger? A hotel owner? A person who often hikes in the woods?

9. Human beings are animals, just like wolves, rabbits, crows and frogs. Each kind of animal has its own way of thinking, behaving and communicating. It is difficult for different animals to know how others think and communicate, or why they behave in different ways.
Since people think in human ways, can people realistically write from an animal's point of view? Can we really understand how an animal thinks and feels or do we give it the feelings that we imagine it would have when we write from its point of view? What do you think?

10. Rewrite one of the *Loon Laughter* stories, or a story of your own, as a radio play. Include the sounds of nature in your production: bird songs, the sound of the wind, rushing water, a wolf's howl. Try to use these sounds to help the listeners understand the story better. For instance, if you were rewriting "The Bison Jump," how would the injured bull's bellow sound? How would the animals' hooves sound as they struck the earth? Try to imagine the entire situation so you will be able to include the noises that will make your radio play sound realistic. After writing the story, try tape

recording it, paying special attention to how you reproduce the sounds of nature.

11.a Several stories in this book illustrate ways that human beings try to control nature – by "improving" trees, changing streams, killing wolves and cutting forests to make room for agriculture and construction. Should people interfere with nature? If so, how much? If not, why not?

11.b Record ways in which people have interfered with nature in your community. For example, road building, home construction and the installation of power lines. For each change you have noted, identify who the change has helped and who it might have harmed. The "who" in this case might be people, animals, plants, a body of water, the soil or the air. Also identify whether or not you think people should have made each change. Should they have interfered with nature in that way? Why or why not?

12. Paul Aird writes, "Two forces shape the world – nature and human nature." Are human nature and nature two *separate* forces? Are nature and human nature *opposing* forces? Should they be? Can you think of anything that people have done that is in opposition to, or against, nature? Or that is cooperative, and works with nature?

List the human activities from the stories in this book that illustrate how people have acted against nature. List the ways in which people have co-operated with, or helped, nature. Which list is longer? Is this a reflection of the way the author writes, or of the way people really act toward nature? Can you explain this?

"Red Fox on a Fence," Thoreau MacDonald, 1941
Lithograph of pencil drawing
From the Thoreau MacDonald Papers, Thomas Fisher Rare Book
Library, University of Toronto

BIOGRAPHY OF PAUL LEET AIRD

Paul Aird is is a lifelong conservationist. He grew up on his family's farm on the shore of the Ottawa River in Hudson, Québec. His education includes an undergraduate degree in agriculture from McGill University and graduate degrees that combine forestry and conservation from Cornell University.

Paul has promoted conservation during his 20 years of work as a forester and forest scientist in the Québec forest industry and then as professor of forest conservation policy in the Faculty of Forestry, University of Toronto. He has also served as a member of the University's Board of Governors and of the Ontario government's Niagara Escarpment Commission.

Paul's travels through forests, fields, rivers and lakes have inspired him to write these stories about Canada's precious natural heritage of wild plants and animals, and about the need to sustain Canada's unique portion of the world's natural environment.

Paul is the author of numerous reports, articles, fables and poems about nature conservation, and is a popular guest speaker. He lives on the Niagara Escarpment in the village of Inglewood, Ontario.

BIOGRAPHY OF THOREAU MACDONALD, 1901-1989

Thoreau MacDonald was born in Toronto, Ontario. His formative years were spent in rural areas near High Park, Toronto, and Thornhill, Ontario. Thoreau's drawings and writings about the wild plants and animals native to these parts reflect his deep concern for and support of nature conservation.

Thoreau has been described as an artist, designer, calligrapher, writer, publisher, farmer, naturalist, nature lover and conservationist. He has created thousands of works including black-and-white pencil, pen and brush drawings, stencils, linocuts, woodcuts, silkscreens, watercolours and oils. He became a master in creating detailed line drawings of natural objects set within their stylized habitats.

Under his Woodchuck Press imprint, Thoreau designed and published sixteen books or booklets of his own. His drawings and calligraphy have adorned hundreds of books written by others. The most notable among these are *Flint and Feather*, E. Pauline Johnson, 1924; *Lyrics of Earth: Sonnets and Ballads*, Archibald Lampman, 1925; *The Chopping Bee and other Laurentian Stories*, Brother Marie Victorin, 1925; *Ateliers: Études sur vingt-deux peintres et sculpteurs canadiens*, Jean Chauvin, 1928; *West by East, and Other Poems*, J.E.H. MacDonald, 1933; *Maria Chapdelaine*, Louis Hémon, translated by W.H. Blake, 1938; *J.E.H. MacDonald: A Biography and Catalogue of his Work*, E.R. Hunter, 1940; *Anne of Green Gables*, Lucy Maud Montgomery, 1942; *David and Other Poems*, Earle Birney, 1942; *Six Trees*, the Canadian Pulp and Paper Association, Montreal, 1951; *The Story of the Group of Seven*, Lawren Harris, 1964; and *Tom*

Thomson: the Algonquin Years, Ottelyn Addison in collaboration with Elizabeth Harwood, 1969.

Significant collections of Thoreau MacDonald's drawings and paintings are held at the University of Toronto, Queen's University, McGill University, Art Gallery of Ontario, Kleinburg's McMichael Canadian Art Collection, Art Gallery of Hamilton, London Regional Art Gallery, National Gallery of Canada, Winnipeg Art Gallery, Vancouver Art Gallery, Upper Canada College in Toronto, Dartmouth College in Hanover, New Hampshire, and the Victoria and Albert Museum, London, England.

Robert Hunter (1942) aptly wrote that Thoreau MacDonald was "a defender of the simple life, and a believer in the right of all things to live in their own way."

Compiled in part from:

Edison, Margaret E. 1973. *Thoreau MacDonald: A Catalogue of Design and Illustration.* Toronto, Ontario: University of Toronto Press.

Flood, John. 1977. "Northern Ontario Art: A Study in Line Drawings. Part I: Thoreau MacDonald." *Boréal* 9:2-11.

Flood, John. 1980. *Thoreau MacDonald's Notebooks,* Moonbeam, Ontario: Penumbra Press.

Hunter, Robert E. 1942. *Thoreau MacDonald.* Toronto, Ontario: Ryerson Press.

Pierce, L. Bruce. 1971. *Thoreau MacDonald: Illustrator, Designer, Observer of Nature.* Toronto, Ontario: Norflex Limited.

Pierce, Lorne. 1942. *Thoreau MacDonald.* Toronto, Ontario: Ryerson Press.

BIOGRAPHY OF CELINA OWEN

CELINA OWEN is Education Co-ordinator at the Ontario Forestry Association where she assists with the research, development and operation of forestry education projects, such as "Envirothon," a hands-on environmental program for high school students. She also writes articles on behalf of the Association for educational and forestry publications.

Celina completed a Bachelor of Arts degree and elementary teacher training at Simon Fraser University in Burnaby, British Columbia, with a primary interest in Communications, English Literature and Sociology. She was a teacher in Surrey, British Columbia, before moving to Ontario.

Emblems Drawn and Printed at the end of books
privately published by Thoreau MacDonald

Printed in *Village & Fields: A Few Country Poems*, J.E.H. MacDonald, Thornhill, Ontario, 1933

Printed in *Birds and Animals, 2nd Series* Thoreau MacDonald, Thornhill, Ontario, 1971

Thoreau translated his Latin motto as,
"Love of country leads me on."